Working
ANIMALS
OF THE WORLD

by Tammy Gagne

raintree
a Capstone company — publishers for children

Raintree is an imprint of Capstone Global Library Limited, a company incorporated in England and Wales having its registered office at 7 Pilgrim Street, London, EC4V 6LB – Registered company number: 6695582

www.raintree.co.uk
myorders@raintree.co.uk

Editorial Credits
Kathryn Clay, editor; Bobbie Nuytten, designer; Jo Miller, media researcher;
Kathy McColley, production specialist

ISBN 978 1 4062 9309 8
18 17 16 15 14
10 9 8 7 6 5 4 3 2 1

British Library Cataloguing in Publication Data
A full catalogue record for this book is available from the British Library.

Photo Credits
Gamma-Rapho via Getty Images: Xavier ROSSI, 9; Getty Images: Photo Researchers/Dr Merlin Tuttle/BCI, 13; Shutterstock: Africa Studio, 12, ajman, 11, Allocricetulus, 20, Dimijana, 5, Dmitri Gomon, cover (top), 1, irin-k, 4 (left), Jody Ann, cover (middle), 15, Johannes Dag Mayer, 14, Kletr, 4 (right), Margaret M Stewart, cover (bottom right), 7, Moize nicolas, 19, Nick Stubbs, 17, PHOTO FUN, cover, Ratikova, 21, wormig, 22 (map)

Every effort has been made to contact copyright holders of material reproduced in this book. Any omissions will be rectified in subsequent printings if notice is given to the publisher.

All the Internet addresses (URLs) given in this book were valid at the time of going to press. However, due to the dynamic nature of the Internet, some addresses may have changed, or sites may have changed or ceased to exist since publication. While the author and publisher regret any inconvenience this may cause readers, no responsibility for any such changes can be accepted by either the author or the publisher.

Printed in China.
0914/CA21401516

Table of Contents

Ladybird

The work animals do naturally often helps humans. An animal's habits, waste and food choices can be useful. Ladybirds can eat up to 50 aphids in a single day. Aphids are small insects that destroy crops. By eating aphids, ladybirds help farmers to keep their crops healthy.

Fact: A ladybird eats more than 5,000 aphids during its lifetime.

5

Frog

Like people, frogs need water to survive. Instead of drinking water, frogs **absorb** it through their skin. They also soak up any chemicals in the water. Healthy frogs are a sign of safe water. If chemicals enter the water, frogs can become ill. When scientists see unhealthy frogs, they know the water is unsafe.

Fact: Australia is home to more than 200 different **species** of frog.

absorb soak up

species group of animals with similar features

7

Giant Pouched Rat

Trained giant pouched rats find forgotten **land mines** in Africa. Their strong sense of smell allows them to sniff out buried bombs. Tiny harnesses keep the rats from running away. Since 2006, giant pouched rats have found more than 2,400 deadly mines.

land mine bomb buried under ground

Fact: At 1 metre (3 feet) long, giant pouched rats are bigger than most domestic cats.

Vulture

Because vultures are **scavengers**, some people think they spread disease. But vultures actually help to prevent diseases such as **rabies** and **cholera**. They eat animals that have died from illnesses before the diseases can spread to humans. Stomach juices kill germs that might otherwise harm the birds.

scavenger animal that feeds on animals that are already dead

rabies deadly disease that people and animals can get from the bite of an infected animal

cholera dangerous disease that causes severe sickness and diarrhoea

Fact: Vultures often eat so much they are too heavy to fly. When this happens, they vomit part of their meal.

Bat

Bats may look scary. But these winged **mammals** help the world in several ways. Gardeners use bat waste as a natural **fertilizer** for their plants. Bat saliva is used in medicine to keep blood flowing instead of clotting.

mammal warm-blooded animal that breathes air; mammals have hair or fur; female mammals feed milk to their young

fertilizer substance added to soil to make crops grow better

Fact: Like ladybirds and frogs, bats eat insects. They can eat up to 1,200 insects in one hour!

Beaver

Beavers are known for chewing trees and making **dams**. They destroy trees, but this behaviour is actually helpful. Beaver dams prevent **droughts** by keeping water in areas that would otherwise be dry. The dams also provide water to help people fight forest fires.

Fact: A beaver dam can measure 3 metres (10 feet) high and more than 50 metres (165 feet) wide.

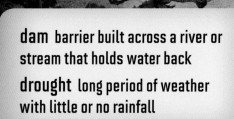

dam barrier built across a river or stream that holds water back

drought long period of weather with little or no rainfall

Dung Beetle

The **dung** beetle's disgusting diet helps to keep the world clean. This insect eats animal waste that could otherwise spread diseases to humans. Dung beetles also bury animal waste. They use the buried waste as food or as a place to lay eggs. Some of the waste is filled with seeds that grow into new plants.

dung solid waste from animals

Fact: Some dung beetles roll dung into balls. Females lay eggs inside the dung balls.

17

Shark

Sharks play an important role at the top of the **food chain**. They eat hundreds of old and unhealthy fish. Removing these fish keeps diseases from spreading to people and other fish. Sharks also keep fish populations from growing too large.

food chain series of organisms in which each one in the series eats the one preceding it

Fact: Sharks are not as dangerous as people think. More than 350 shark species exist. But only about 30 species are dangerous to humans.

Bee

Bees do more than make honey. They carry **pollen** from one part of a plant to another. Moving the pollen helps new plants to grow. Bees help farmers to produce about one-third of everything we eat. They also have an excellent sense of smell. People can train bees to find cancer, chemicals and gunpowder.

pollen powder made by flowers to help them create new seeds

Habitat Map

Animals' locations by continent:

North America:
Bat
Beaver
Bee
Dung Beetle
Frog
Ladybird
Vulture

South America:
Bat
Bee
Dung Beetle
Frog
Ladybird

Africa:
Bee
Dung Beetle
Frog
Giant Pouched Rat
Ladybird

Europe:
Bee
Dung Beetle
Frog
Ladybird

Asia:
Bee
Dung Beetle
Frog
Ladybird

Australia:
Bee
Dung Beetle
Frog
Ladybird

Oceans:
Sharks

Glossary

absorb soak up

cholera dangerous disease that causes severe sickness and diarrhoea

dam barrier built across a river or stream that holds water back

drought long period of weather with little or no rainfall

dung solid waste from animals

fertilizer substance added to soil to make crops grow better

food chain series of organisms in which each one in the series eats the one preceding it

land mine bomb buried under ground

mammal warm-blooded animal that breathes air; mammals have hair or fur; female mammals feed milk to their young

pollen powder made by flowers to help them create new seeds

rabies deadly disease that people and animals can get from the bite of an infected animal

scavenger animal that feeds on animals that are already dead

species group of animals with similar features

Comprehension Questions

1. Reread page 18 about how sharks keep fish populations from growing too large. What might happen if fish populations grew too large?

2. In what ways can animals prevent the spread of disease?

23

Books

Animal Heroes (War Stories), Jane Bingham (Raintree, 2012)

Amazing Animal Helpers (Animal Superpowers), John Townsend (Raintree, 2013)

Bees and Wasps (Usborne Beginners), James Maclaine (Usborne Publishing Ltd, 2013)

Websites

www.ngkids.co.uk/did-you-know/Honey-Bees
Learn 10 facts about honey bees and view pictures of honey bees.

www.fun-facts.org.uk/animals/animals-frog.htm
Learn about frogs, including their diet, life cycle and information about species of frog.

Index